Inhaltsverzeichnis

Musterlösungen   20

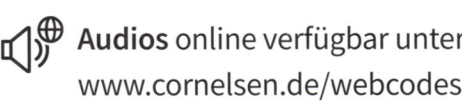

Audios online verfügbar unter
www.cornelsen.de/webcodes   **Code:** vawobi

W0236754

FACT FILE: NEW ZEALAND

New Zealand (NZ) consists of two big islands and hundreds of small islands. The two main islands are called North Island
5 and South Island. New Zealand is about the same size as the United Kingdom, but only 5 million people live there. Its closest neighbour is
10 Australia – 2000 km away!

The country's capital is Wellington. It's on the southern end of North Island. Most New Zealanders live in
15 Auckland, the biggest city. To buy things in New Zealand, you need New Zealand dollars (NZ$).

The official languages are
20 English, Māori and New Zealand sign language. The Māori are the indigenous people of New Zealand, which means they were the first
25 people there. The main ethnic groups in New Zealand today are Europeans, Māori, Asians and people from the Pacific Islands.

New Zealand is an independent country, but its head of state is the King of England.
30 New Zealand's flag has the flag of the United Kingdom in the top left corner.

New Zealand's flag

ENGLISH G

LIGHTHOUSE | HEADLIGHT | HIGHLIGHT

New Zealand
Facts and Texts

 Audio online

Cornelsen

New Zealand: Facts and Texts
LIGHTHOUSE | HEADLIGHT | HIGHLIGHT

Erarbeitet in der Redaktion von: Klaus Unger (Projektleitung);

Uta Dittmann (verantwortliche Redakteurin), Brianna Gorman

Auf der Grundlage von Arbeiten folgender Autorinnen und Autoren: Marc Proulx, Sydney Thorne

Layout-Konzept und Umschlaggestaltung: Klein & Halm, Berlin

Layout und technische Umsetzung: Straive

Titelbild

Mt. Ngauruhoe, Tongariro National Park, New Zealand: stock.adobe.com/NMint (Ausschnitt)

Abbildungen

S. 2 New Zealand map: Cornelsen/Carlos Borrell Eiköter, flag: Shutterstock.com/ymcgraphic; S. 3 ob. li.: mauritius images/alamy stock photo/Douglas Fisher, ob. re.: Shutterstock.com/Pi-Lens, Mitte li.: Shutterstock.com/Jiri Prochazka, Mitte re.: Shutterstock.com/Roberto Dani ; S. 4 ob. re.: Shutterstock.com/Sivad, un. li.: Shutterstock.com/Matias Dandrea; S. 5: Shutterstock.com/Emagnetic; S. 7 ob.: Shutterstock.com/Kanuman, Mitte: Shutterstock.com/josh.tagi, un.: Shutterstock.com/wavebreakmedia; S. 8 ob.: mauritius images/alamy stock photo/Molly Marshall, Mitte: Shutterstock.com/HeliHead, un. (backpack): stock.adobe.com/fotofabrika; S.10: Shutterstock.com/Rawpixel.com; S. 11 stock.adobe.com/lcrribeiro33@gmail; S. 13: Shutterstock.com/photocosmos1; S. 14 li.: Shutterstock.com/Dmitry Naumov, re.: mauritius images/alamy stock photo/Andre M. Chang; S. 15: Shutterstock.com/Jakub Cejpek; S. 17: Shutterstock.com/Maksym Dykha; S. 18: stock.adobe.com/dudlajzov; S. 19: Shutterstock.com/Molly NZ; S. 20 New Zealand map: Cornelsen/Carlos Borrell Eiköter

www.cornelsen.de

Soweit in diesem Lehrwerk Personen fotografisch abgebildet sind und ihnen von der Redaktion fiktive Namen, Berufe, Dialoge und Ähnliches zugeordnet oder diese Personen in bestimmte Kontexte gesetzt werden, dienen diese Zuordnungen und Darstellungen ausschließlich der Veranschaulichung und dem besseren Verständnis des Inhalts.

1. Auflage, 1. Druck 2023

© 2023 Cornelsen Verlag GmbH, Berlin

Druck: Athesiadruck GmbH

ISBN: 978-3-06-036658-3

The Māori people came to New Zealand about 300 years before the Europeans. *Kia ora,* the Māori word for 'Hi', is now used by lots of New Zealanders.

New Zealand has an incredibly beautiful coast, spectacular lakes and mountains. It has amazing geysers, like the Pohutu Geyser, which is in action once an hour.

The Kiwi bird is a national icon of New Zealand. It can't fly and does look a bit like a kiwi fruit, right? Kiwi is also the nickname for New Zealanders.

In New Zealand, you can still find plants and animals which have existed for millions of years. The Tuatara is the last of its kind and is a protected species. Nearly a third of New Zealand is protected by national parks and marine reserves.

1 Mark New Zealand's capital and its biggest city on the map.

2 New Zealand quiz: Write the correct answers.

   A What is the name of the indigenous people? _____

   B What is the nickname for New Zealanders? _____

   C How do you say 'Hi' in the Māori language? _____

   D Name the three things a kiwi can be. _____

   E Who is New Zealand's head of state? _____

   F What are the two main parts of New Zealand? _____

- First read the text.
- Then do the tasks (1 – 9).
- For tasks 1, 6 and 8, tick the correct box and quote from the text.
- For tasks 2, 3, 4, 7 and 9 tick the correct box.
- For task 5, fill in the information.

The land of the long white cloud

About 800 years ago, there were no people living in New Zealand at all. It was a land of primeval forests[1] and birds, many of which couldn't fly. They
5 survived easily because there weren't many animals hunting them.

In the late 13th century, people from the Polynesian islands in the Pacific Ocean saw the land from their canoes. In
10 their language, they said what they saw: Aotearoa – land of the long white cloud.

Māori settlement

The people in their boats were Māori people. They liked Aotearoa and came to settle on the two big islands. They grew
15 food in their gardens, ate fish and big flightless birds. They also developed their own individual Māori culture creating art, making tools and weapons.

The long white cloud over New Zealand

The Māori were living like that for
20 nearly 400 years, when the first Europeans arrived in the 17th century. The first settlers named the country Nova Zeeland, after a province of the Netherlands. The British then called it
25 New Zealand.

The Europeans, most of whom where British, began to settle on the islands. They hunted seals and whales and traded their products with the
30 Māori. As more and more Europeans came to settle, however, conflict and violence over Māori land began.

The Treaty of Waitangi

The Māori weren't happy. They asked the British government for protection,
35 which Britain promised to give - under the condition that the Māori enter into an agreement with them, known as the Treaty of Waitangi.

Under the Treaty, the British
40 government guaranteed the Māori ownership of their land and protection

Māori art: faces carved into tree trunks

---

[1] *primeval forest*: Urwald

against aggressors. In return, the Māori had to recognize New Zealand as a British colony and Britain as their ruler. 45 The Treaty was signed at Waitangi on 6 February 1840.

Formally regulating the relationship between the Māori and Europeans, the Treaty of Waitangi is considered New 50 Zealand's founding document today. 6 February, or Waitangi Day, is now New Zealand's national holiday.

European colonialism

With the Treaty, New Zealand became a British colony. More and more British 55 immigrants came to settle, but in many cases, the promises made in the Treaty of Waitangi weren't kept. During periods of violent conflict, the British took large parts of Māori land.

Colonial-style buildings: a reminder of British colonialism in New Zealand

60 A lot of violations[2] of the Treaty of Waitangi have still not been compensated for. A tribunal has been set up to compensate Māori for the injustices of the colonial period, but a lot remains 65 to be made up for.

With British colonialism in New Zealand, the non-Māori, or *Pākehā* population increased, diminishing the Māori, their culture and achievements. As 70 Māori culture was disappearing more and more, New Zealand's landscape changed too: the British burnt down large parts of primeval forest to provide fields for farming. Agriculture, especially sheep 75 farming, became an important part of the economy. Although New Zealand still has great biodiversity today, it is much impoverished compared to Māori times.

In spite of the damage the British 80 had done to New Zealand nature, a deep respect for nature is what unites all its people today – Māori, European descendants, Asians and Pacific islanders. As problems remain, efforts 85 are made to come to terms with past injustices. New Zealand is now considered a bi-cultural country, with equal rights for everyone. The Māori greeting 'Kia ora' is commonly used by 90 all groups of the population, showing mutual respect and concern.

---

[2] *violation*: Vertragsverletzung

---

1 Before the Māori came to New Zealand, it was a paradise for birds.

This statement is ☐ true ☐ false ... because the text says ...

---

2 When the Māori first set eyes on New Zealand, they saw ...

a) ☐ a lot of flightless birds.

b) ☐ a long white cloud.

c) ☐ pretty gardens with flowers and vegetables.

3 Most of the European settlers in New Zealand came from ...

a) ☐ the Netherlands.

b) ☐ the Pacific islands.

c) ☐ Britain.

4 The Treaty of Waitangi is ...

a) ☐ an agreement between Britain and New Zealand.

b) ☐ a Māori tradition.

c) ☐ New Zealand's national holiday.

5 What are the two main agreements made in the Treaty of Waitangi?

1 The British ...

_____

2 The Māori ...

_____

6 A tribunal ensured that all Māori were compensated for the injustices of the past.

This statement is ☐ true ☐ false because the text says ...

_____

7 Since the arrival of the British colonialists, New Zealand's landscape changed a lot because ...

a) ☐ the British needed a lot of tea plantations.

b) ☐ forests were burnt to make space for farming.

c) ☐ pollution caused climate change.

8 There is hardly any biodiversity in New Zealand since the British colonialists came.

This statement is ☐ true ☐ false because the text says ...

_____

9 When people use the Māori greeting 'Kia ora', it shows ...

a) ☐ that they can speak foreign languages.

b) ☐ respect for each other and Māori history.

c) ☐ that they grew up in a Māori family.

2 READING Lina's New Zealand blog

- First look at the pictures in Lina's blog and discuss with a partner: Why has Lina posted these pictures? What's the story behind them?
- Then read the texts and do the tasks 1 – 8.
- For tasks 1, 2, 3, 5 and 8, tick the correct box.
- For tasks 4, 6 and 7, tick the correct box and quote from the text.

I'm now a volunteer at Don and Anna's organic farm on South Island. This is their flock of sheep. They have a total of 436 sheep! Great view, ey? I'm learning
5 lots of new skills here. Tomorrow I'm going to work with the animals. So, watch out guys – if I get a chance when I'm home I'll show you how to milk a goat! 😊

10 Today was one of the best of all! I joined a group in Queenstown and together with a guide we walked down a river. Easy, do I hear you say? You have no idea! Kitted out in wetsuits, helmets and life
15 jackets, we climbed down waterfalls, flew over the river on zip wires, jumped into deep water, swam a bit and even explored some caves. It was an adventure and then some!

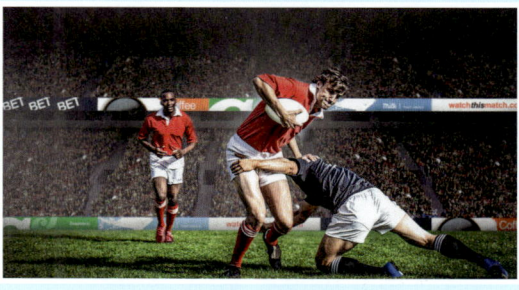

20 I took this photo today. Rugby is a wild game and it's incredibly popular here. With a population of only 5 million, New Zealand is one of the top countries in the world at rugby – how amazing is that?

25
30

Kia Ora everybody! Today I went on a tour of Auckland with Tai and Nikau, my Māori guides. They told me that lots of places in New Zealand have Māori names. Like Takapuna – the part of Auckland where my hostel is. Nikau also told me that tattoos are important in Māori culture because they are a sign of a person's identity. It was a great tour. I love meeting local people when I travel. Tomorrow they are going to take me to Whangarei. If we're lucky, we might see kiwi birds there!!

35
40

I'm still feeling a bit tired after two long-haul flights: 6 hours from Munich to Dubai and 17 hours from Dubai to Auckland! I knew that Auckland is New Zealand's biggest city, so I expected the high-rise buildings and the busy city centre. But I was surprised by Auckland's great beaches and about 50 volcanoes! I want to climb one of them tomorrow! And I might try the outside walk 192 metres up around Auckland's Sky Tower. It looks awesome. You can even do a Skyjump from the tower – but I won't do that!

45

Hi guys, welcome to my New Zealand blog! I'm leaving tomorrow, and I'm so excited! A whole year to travel New Zealand! I'll keep you posted right here!

Numbers

1 5,000,000 is the number …

a) ☐ of sheep on South Island.

b) ☐ of flights from Dubai per year.

c) ☐ of people living in New Zealand.

2 12 …

a) ☐ months is how long Lina is going to travel around New Zealand.

b) ☐ is the number of tattoos a traditional Māori person has.

c) ☐ hours is how long Lina travelled from Munich to Auckland.

3 23 …

a) ☐ hours is how long Lina spent up in the air when travelling to New Zealand.

b) ☐ rugby players are always on the field during a game.

c) ☐ kilogram in luggage is what you are allowed on a long-haul flight.

4 Auckland's Sky Tower is 192 metres high.

This statement is ☐ true ☐ false   because the text says …

_____

About New Zealand

5 Queenstown is a good place …

a) ☐   for adventure sports out in nature.

b) ☐   if you like cats.

c) ☐   for guided sightseeing tours.

6 New Zealand is one of the best countries at rugby in the world.

This statement is ☐ true ☐ false   because the text says …

_____

7 You can easily find kiwi birds everywhere in New Zealand.

This statement is ☐ true ☐ false   because the text says …

_____

8 Auckland …

a) ☐   is the capital of New Zealand.

b) ☐   has no airport.

c) ☐   is New Zealand's largest city.

3 **WRITING**

- Read Lina's blog again. Consider: What do you find interesting? Have you got any questions for Lina?
- Read Tom's comment and then write your own comment below.

I'm so jealous of you, Lina! You are having fun in New Zealand while I have to go to school for one more year! Your adventure in Queenstown sounds amazing. I'm also really interested in the Māori culture, tell us more about that! And keep us updated about your great experiences, PLEASE!!!
Tom

Your comment

_____

_____

_____

- First read the text.
- Then do the tasks 1–5.
- For task 1, tick the correct box and fill in the information.
- For tasks 2 and 5, tick the correct box and quote from the text.
- For task 3, fill in the information.
- For task 4, tick the correct box.

Kendra Williams, 16, remembers her first introduction to rugby: 'I was little – maybe four. We had watched our dad play in a game, and my brother Cole and
5 I ran around the garden with a rugby ball, tackling each other and laughing our heads off.'

At the Williams' home in Masterton, a North-Island town east of the
10 capital Wellington, Kendra points to the three framed photos in the hall that suggest a long history of rugby in this family.

'That's my great-grandfather with
15 the local Rugby Union club. That was 1952. The second picture is Dad when he played for his Wellington club, and that's me at school when we won the regional cup.'
20 The love of rugby runs deep here. For anyone who wants to understand New Zealand culture, rugby is a good place to start. Americans have baseball, Britons have soccer (or football) and New
25 Zealanders have rugby. It's the most watched, played and talked about sport in the country. It's also an integral part of Kiwi culture and identity.

Rugby is a team sport that is played
30 in more than 120 countries around the world. It was brought here from England in the 1870s and quickly caught on. Community grassroots rugby – in

The girls' team huddle before the match starts.

schools, clubs and provincial teams – is
35 strong in New Zealand. Thanks to the great commitment in our communities', the All Blacks and the Black Ferns – the men's and women's national teams – are the most feared opponents in
40 international competition.

On any Saturday nationwide, players big and small put on their gear and run onto rugby fields to play school and club rugby. Small-town rugby clubs,
45 like in Masterton, are often the hub of the community and a venue for social gatherings.

Even famous All Blacks players keep strong ties with their community
50 clubs and spend time playing and giving workshops and camps locally.

Historian Ian Goode explains the importance of the sport in the national psyche: 'Our country was still very young when the game first arrived here. We didn't know yet what it meant to be New Zealanders.' Rugby became popular both with the European settlers and the indigenous Māori.

Rugby is a very physical game.

60   This gritty, physical contact sport appealed to the tough farming mentality and the Māori warrior ideals.

    In 1905 the first national rugby team, the Original All Blacks, toured the
65 British Isles and France. It was a turning point. 'They won every game except one controversial game against Wales,' Goode says. 'It was impressive – a huge achievement. We showed the world
70 that this small island nation could be the best at something. Those players became national heroes. Since then, rugby has been a part of who we are as a country.'

75   The Māori and Pacific Islander players, with their characteristic strength, speed and love of the game, helped shape rugby in New Zealand.

    The game became a way for the
80 country's different groups to mix and connect. From the beginning, the All Blacks adopted the haka – the Māori war dance – as a ritual before each game. Performed together by Māori and
85 Pākehā players, it's a powerful image.

The national teams are a source of pride for everyone in this rugby-loving nation.

    On a cool, sunny Saturday morning in Masterton, the under-13s (the 'Small
90 Blacks') have finished their game and now watch from the sidelines as Kendra Williams leads her club against regional rivals Porirua.

    A crowd of proud parents shout
95 support from the sidelines. Later, after Kendra and her teammates have celebrated their win and the teams have shaken hands, the activity on the sidelines continues with players chatting, children
100 playing and parents networking and talking.

    Kendra, her face dirty with mud, pushes her hair back and thinks about the future: 'Whether I make it to the Black
105 Ferns or not, I'll always come back here.'

---

1 Rugby is important mainly to certain parts of New Zealand society.

This statement is ☐ true ☐ false.   Give one or two reasons why.

_____

_____

2 Kendra is the first in her family to play rugby.

This statement is ☐ true ☐ false   because the text says …

_____

_____

3 What are New Zealand's two national Rugby teams called? Who plays in them?

_____

_____

4 Community-level rugby...

a) ☐ plays a minor role in New Zealand.

b) ☐ brings together all sorts of people.

c) ☐ is for boys only.

5 The Māori didn't like Rugby very much at first.

This statement is ☐ true ☐ false because the text says ...

_____

5 WORDS Article or no article?

- Do the tasks 1 – 6.
- For tasks 1 – 5, fill in 'the' where necessary. If no 'the' is needed fill in '-'.
- For task 6, write one sentence with each noun and decide if 'the' is needed or not.

1 Kendra's rugby career began at _____ home in the garden.

2 _____ people in Kendra's town are big fans of hers.

3 The game is simply a part of _____ culture in New Zealand.

4 Kendra still goes to _____ school in Masterton.

5 Kiwis love _____ sports in general – not just rugby.

6 Write sentences with these nouns:

home _____

people _____

culture _____

school _____

sport _____

6 LISTENING Jacinda Ardern – a leader for our time

- First read the tips for listening tasks.
- Then read the tasks.
- Then listen to the story.
- While you are listening, tick the correct box.
- At the end, you will hear the interview again.

TIPS FOR LISTENING TASKS
- The words used in the answers are often not the exact words that you hear.
For example: instead of 'well known' you hear 'still unknown'; instead of 'argue' you hear 'express her views'.
- When the answer isn't immediately clear, decide which answers are definitely wrong. Then you only need to choose one of the answers that are left.
- Words or phrases in the listening text are often replaced with synonyms (words with the same meaning) or antonyms (words with the opposite meaning) in the answers. Think about synonyms and antonyms of key words in your tasks.

1 When Jacinda Ardern became a member of parliament in 2008, …
a) ☐ she was already well known.
b) ☐ she could argue clearly and get people's attention.
c) ☐ she was just 25 years old.
d) ☐ she was the first woman in parliament.

Jacinda Ardern, New Zealand's prime minister

2 'Jacindamania' actually began …
a) ☐ before she became Labour Party leader.
b) ☐ despite negative news reports.
c) ☐ before she became prime minister.
d) ☐ although the media ignored her.

3 When the prime minister became pregnant, …
a) ☐ she had to choose between work and family.
b) ☐ even her critics supported her.
c) ☐ continuing her job, she said, was unacceptable.
d) ☐ she made it clear that she would continue her job.

4 As prime minister, Jacinda Ardern …
a) ☐ was slow to react after the terrorist attack.
b) ☐ spoke to the public weekly during the pandemic.
c) ☐ encouraged people to be nice to each other.
d) ☐ is known for being cold and unfriendly.

- First read the text.
- Then do tasks 1–10.
- For task 1, choose the correct title for each paragraph. Write the title on the line above the paragraph.
- For tasks 2 and 9, tick the correct box.
- For tasks 3, 6, 7 and 8, tick the correct box and quote from the text.
- For tasks 4, 5 and 10, fill in the information.

Christchurch, the largest city on New Zealand's South Island, has always been thought of as a quiet place where not much happens. Wellington, though
5 smaller, has the buzz of a capital city, a busy ferry terminal and a centre of excellence in the international film industry. Auckland, with almost two fifths of its population born overseas, is
10 one of the most diverse cities in the world. The country's business centre, it is also within easy reach of the country's awesome geysers and steaming mud pools in Rotorua.

The river Avon runs peacefully through Christchurch.

15   But Christchurch? Its title as New Zealand's Garden City is hardly dramatic. While Auckland and Wellington are surrounded by volcanoes, Christchurch lies among the fields of the Canterbury

20 Plain – great for farming, but low on the country's list of dramatic scenery. And while Queenstown, over on the west coast, offers jetboating, skydiving and an exciting luge[1] track, Christchurch is
25 famous for punting – a sport in which you drop a long pole into the river, push against it and move a boat gently along the river. It is surely the quietest, slowest and least exciting water sport in the
30 world.

      But the city's hills and gardens don't tell the whole story. For Christchurch lies on the Ring of Fire, a line that goes up America's west coast,
35 down the east coast of Asia, and then – missing Australia – swings across to

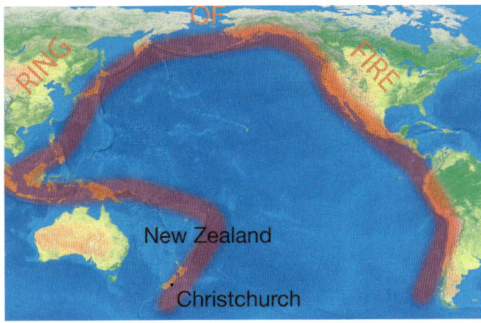

New Zealand. Most of the world's earthquakes take place along this line, and Christchurch, too, has a history of
40 earthquakes. There were minor earthquakes in the nineteenth century,

[1] luge: rodeln, Rodel-

for example, and an earthquake in 2010 injured two people and destroyed a small number of buildings.

_____

45 All the same, nobody was prepared for the earthquake that shook the city at lunchtime on Tuesday, 22nd February 2011. Though no stronger than an earthquake of the year before, its 50 epicentre was more central and so it was more deadly. It was the country's second worst natural disaster after the Hawke's Bay earthquake. 185 people were killed, 130 of them in a six-storey office block 55 that collapsed. Thousands more were injured. The Anglican cathedral lost half

This cathedral in Christchurch was severely damaged in the 2011 earthquake.

of its tower and some of its walls were so weakened that they fell in further earthquakes later the same year. The 60 city's second tallest building was so badly damaged that it had to be taken down later. Hundreds of family homes were damaged and almost 80 per cent of the buildings in the city's CBD (Central 65 Business District) were destroyed.

_____

In most countries, land in a city's CBD is so expensive that it is rebuilt after a disaster. But in an under-populated country such as New Zealand, a number 70 of businesses that had been hit by the earthquake found space for their new offices on the outer edge of the city. This left a large area of unused land in the city centre and the city has tried to find a 75 mix of creative uses for it. The new Riverside Market, for example, is a huge food hall where producers sell their fruit, vegetables, meat and seafood in market stalls, shops, cafes and restaurants. 80 Together with a new library housed in an impressive new building, it is designed to attract the crowds back into the CBD.

1 Match the titles with the paragraphs in the text. Write the titles on the lines above the paragraphs. Two titles don't fit.

New attractions	The day after the disaster
A dangerous zone	The disaster
A tourist centre	Find your own food
Three rival cities	A quiet sort of place

2 According to the text, Auckland ...

a) ☐ has lots of banks and big companies.

b) ☐ is situated a long way from Rotorua.

c) ☐ has two fifths of the population of Christchurch.

3 Wellington, New Zealand's capital, is the largest city in New Zealand.

This statement is ☐ true ☐ false because the text says ...

4 Do you think the author likes Christchurch very much?

Write down words and phrases from the text, which make you think so.

5 Why is Auckland a diverse multicultural city?

6 Christchurch is known for its dramatic scenery.

This statement is ☐ true ☐ false because the text says ...

7 Australia is luckier than New Zealand, as far as earthquakes are concerned.

This statement is ☐ true ☐ false because the text says ...

8 The earthquake in February 2011 caused a lot more damage than an earthquake in 2010.

This statement is ☐ true ☐ false because the text says ...

9 As a result of the earthquake ...

a) ☐ there are new opportunities in the city centre.

b) ☐ land has become more expensive.

c) ☐ the city has no more libraries.

10 How has Christchurch's city centre changed since the 2011 earthquake? Give at least two examples.

8 WORDS Meaning in context

- Read the text again.
- Look for the English words and decide which of the German translations are correct in the context.

busy (line 6)
a) ☐ beschäftigt (Adj.)
b) ☐ arbeitsreich (Adj.)
c) ☐ belebt, geschäftig (Adj.)
d) ☐ besetzt (Adj.)

track (line 24)
a) ☐ Weg, Pfad (N)
b) ☐ Gleis (N)
c) ☐ Bahn, Rennbahn (N)
d) ☐ verfolgen (V)

drop (line 26)
a) ☐ fallen (V)
b) ☐ herablassen (V)
c) ☐ Tropfen (N)
d) ☐ weglassen (V)

plain (line 20)
a) ☐ einfach, schlicht (Adj.)
b) ☐ klar (Adj.)
c) ☐ halbbitter (Adj.)
d) ☐ Ebene (N)

hit (line 70)
a) ☐ schlagen (V)
b) ☐ treffen (V)
c) ☐ Schlag, Stoß, Treffer (N)
d) ☐ Erfolg, Hit (N)

9 LISTENING

- First read tasks 1 – 4.
- Then listen to the interview.
- While you are listening, tick the correct boxes.
- At the end you will hear the interview again.
- Finally, do task 5.
- Read the questions and discuss with your classmates.
- Now listen to the interview and do the tasks.

9.1 A long walk

1 Dustin's adventure ...
a) ☐ started on South Island.
b) ☐ began when he was 17.
c) ☐ was a 3,000-kilometre trek.

2 His journey was inspired by ...
a) ☐ his best mate.
b) ☐ a book.
c) ☐ a dream.

3 The biggest lesson for him was ...
a) ☐ learning who he was and what he wanted.
b) ☐ that people are kind and generous.
c) ☐ to trust that everything will be okay.

4 During his travels, Dustin ...
a) ☐ only slept outdoors.
b) ☐ never used a phone.
c) ☐ hunted and ate different animals.

5 **Discuss:** Would you like to go on a trek like Dustin? Why? Why not?

Where would you like to do this?
What could be difficult? What could you do about it?

Travelling New Zealand by yourself
- An unforgettable experience

9.2 The influence of Māori culture

- First read the tasks.
- Then listen to the podcast.
- While you are listening, tick the correct boxes and/ or write down the information.
- At the end you will hear the podcast again.
- Now listen to the podcast and do the tasks.

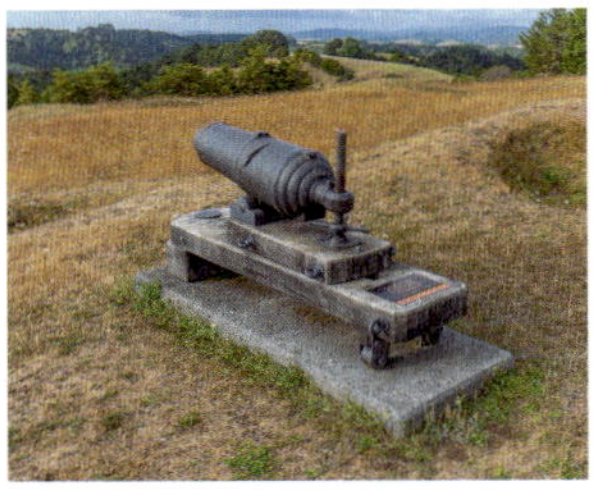

This canon at Ruapekapeka was used in armed conflict between the British forces and the Māori.

1 The Treaty of Waitangi was an agreement between ...

____

2 Pākehā means ...

a) ☐ European culture in New Zealand.

b) ☐ European, Asian, and other cultures in New Zealand that are not Māori.

c) ☐ Māori culture.

3 The treaty is important for the Māori today.

This statement is ☐ true ☐ false because Tim says ...

____

4 In the years after the treaty was signed ...

a) ☐ the land issues between Māori and the Pākehā were solved.

b) ☐ the Pākehā ignored the agreement.

c) ☐ the British left New Zealand.

5 Change came in the 1970s.

This statement is ☐ true ☐ false because Louisa says ...

____

6 As an official language, Te Reo Māori is used ... (2 details)

____

7 The haka is one New Zealand custom that comes from Māori culture. Another is ...

____

8 Louisa Te Awa mentions the town of Rotorua because ...

____

- Read the tasks carefully.
- Write complete sentences.
- Make sure you write about all the aspects presented in each task.

Ataahua, a student in a New Zealand school, wrote this text for her school magazine.

Racism – what can you do?

Racism can be horrible and deadly, like when a white man killed 51 people in two mosques in Christchurch in 2019. We often feel helpless when we see
5 racism like that.

But there is also everyday racism, and we can definitely do something about that. I mean racist jokes, like when a police helicopter flies over my school
10 and the students in my class look at me and say, 'Ataahua, they're coming for you!' They think it's funny, but it isn't – because I know that they're saying it because lots of people think 'All Māoris
15 are criminals'.

Sometimes, new teachers don't even try to say my name correctly. Each time, they're telling me and the class that I'm not important. That hurts. There
20 are teachers who make me feel like I can't achieve good results – even when I don't make any mistakes. They're not even giving me a chance, and that really hurts.
25 If you do want to fight racism, start with yourself. Don't make racist jokes.

Think about what you want to say before you say it. How would you feel if you were in the other person's shoes?
30 Remember that names *are* important, so say them correctly – they're part of a person's identity.

Respect people for what they are, not what they look like or who their
35 parents are. Don't believe everything that people say. Think for yourself, remember that we're all human beings and that we all have the same feelings.

One step at a time, we can make it if
40 we listen to each other and help each other along the way. Let's stick together and leave no room for racism.
Ataahua

1 **Summarize** what Ataahua's post is about.
What is the text's topic? What are her main points?

2 **Explain** the situations in which Ataahua feels she is a victim of racism.

3 **You have a choice here. Choose one of the following tasks.**

A 'If you want to fight racism, start with yourself.'

Comment on this statement from your point of view and include the following aspects:
- reasons in favour of and against this statement
- examples to support your arguments
- what you can do and what you already do to fight racism

or

B Racism – what can you do?

Write an alternative beginning which could replace the first two paragraphs in Ataahua's post. Include the following aspects:
- a suitable opening sentence
- an example of racism which has been on the news and how you and your friends felt about it
- examples of everyday racism in your school, daily life, sports or other areas, which you have experienced yourself or you have heard about from other people
- a short explanation why these are examples of racism

Musterlösungen

Fact file

1

2 A Māori B Kiwi C Kia ora D a bird, a fruit, a person from New Zealand E The King of England F South Island and North Island

1 The history of New Zealand
1 true (l 4) 2 b 3 c 4 a
5 1 The British guaranteed the Māori ownership of their land and protection 2 The Māori had to recognize New Zealand as a British colony and Britain as their ruler.
6 false (l 63–65, 67–68) 7 b 8 false (l 79–80) 9 b

2 Lina's New Zealand blog
Numbers
1 c 2 a 3 a

About New Zealand
4 false (l 41–42) – The tower is higher than the platform you can walk on. 5 a 6 true (l 22–24) 7 false – "If we're lucky, we might see kiwi birds." 8 c

3 Writing
Lösungsbeispiel: I agree, your walk down the river sounds super exciting, but I would love to do the Skyjump too! I'm going to New Zealand next month and I definitely want to do lots of exciting things. I'm looking forward to your next posts for inspiration! PS: Have you seen any kiwi birds yet?

4 More than a game
1 false – It is for everyone and it's the most popular sport in NZ./ "The game became a way for the country's different groups to mix and connect."/ Rugby is popular with everyone and there are teams for men and women, girls and boys./ It brings together everyone and "is an integral part of Kiwi culture and identity." 2 false – (l 11–12, 13–18) 3 The All Blacks is the men's national team and the Black Ferns is the women's national team. 4 b 5 false (l 53–58)

5 Words
1 – 2 the 3 the 4 – 5 –
6 Lösungsbeispiel: She wasn't at **home** when I called./ Buckingham Palace is the **home** of the British monarch. | **People** around the world play rugby./ The **people** in New Zealand love rugby. | Sport and **culture**

are related. / The **culture** of New Zealand is related to rugby. / I always go to **school** by bike. / The **school** is close to my home. | **Sport** is a healthy free-time activity./ The **sport** that I like best is swimming.

6 Jacinda Ardern – a leader for our time
1b 2a 3d 4c

7 Christchurch and its earthquakes
1 Three rival cities – A quiet sort of place – A dangerous zone – The disaster – New attractions – Find your own food 2a 3 false (l 4–5) 4 No. (l 15–16, 20–21, 28–30) 5 (l 8–9) 6 false (l 20–21) 7 true (l 36) 8 true (l 48–51) 9 a 10 (l 71–72, 75–81)

8 Words
busy c) plain d) track c) hit b) drop b)

9 Listening
9.1 A long walk

1c 2b 3a 4c 5 individuell: Klassengespräch

10 Racism – what can you do?
1 Lösungsbeispiel: Ataahua's post is about everyday racism and what everyone can do about it. A Māori girl, Ataahua explains a few examples of everyday racism. She says that when her classmates say things about Māori they think are funny, it's racism because their jokes are based on prejudice.
She also points out that teachers are sometimes racist too, for example when they don't even try to say her name correctly or when they think she can't get good results before they even get to know her.
Her last and main point is that everyone can help to fight racism by starting with themselves. We should respect everyone and accept them as they are.

2 The first situation that Ataahua describes as racism is when police helicopters fly over their school and her classmates joke that the police are looking for her. She explains that this hurts her because the 'joke' is based on the idea that all Māori are criminals, which is a prejudice and not true.
Then she tells us that new teachers sometimes don't even try to pronounce her name correctly. This makes her feel as if she doesn't matter and that hurts her. She also writes that some teachers think she can't get good marks, even when she does everything correctly. Not getting a chance from her teachers is very painful for her.

3a Starting with yourself before criticising others is always a good idea. Campaigning for others to change can take a long time, but you can start today if you want to change yourself.
This is true when fighting racism too but it's also important to speak up when others become victims of racism. Sometimes people say racist things without thinking about it and then someone has to tell them

3b When we hear about horrible racist attacks on the news, for example when a man killed nine people in two shisha bars in Hanau, we are shocked and angry and ask how such things could happen.
If we don't want such horrible acts of racism to happen again, we must recognize racism in everyday life and do something about that. Don't make racist jokes like when we are talking about drugs in class, and a classmate says we should invite my father because he can tell us a lot about it. She thought it was funny, but it hurt so much because there are still so many people who think all black people sell or consume marijuana.
Or when people think they are being nice and tell me that my German is very good. I was born in Germany, and my mother is German! Why shouldn't I speak German? I know they don't mean any harm, but it still hurts because the 'compliment' is based on the idea that someone with dark skin like me can't speak German.

that they are being racist and that it's not okay. For example, my grandfather used to say that he felt sorry for his neighbours' daughter because her parents chose her husband for her and brought him to Germany from Turkey. My sister and I never believed this and always argued with our granddad. We told him to get to know them and ask about their daughter, but he said he couldn't speak to them because they didn't speak German. My sister and I kept telling him that he was wrong and after a while, he stopped his comments. When he once did meet his neighbours, he talked to them and found out that they spoke German perfectly. They told him that their daughter is in a relationship with a German man and that they have a child together but aren't married. So his prejudices about a Turkish family were clearly wrong. We are still quite proud that we kept arguing with our granddad and that he now even says nice things about his Turkish neighbours.
When one of my friends or classmates says racist things, I always try to speak up and tell them that it's not right. This is quite hard sometimes, but then I think about the victims and how much harder it is for them.
To sum up, I think we can improve things for everyone if we start with ourselves and consider the feelings of other people before we say things that may hurt them. But we also have to stand up against racism to show that racism is not okay and that we are all just people.

Cornelsen

ISBN 978-3-06-036658-3

9 783060 366583